SACRAMENT OF BODIES

African
POETRY
BOOK SERIES

Series editor: Kwame Dawes

SACRAMENT
OF BODIES

Romeo Oriogun

University of Nebraska Press / Lincoln

Acknowledgments for the use of copyrighted
material appear on page 63, which constitutes
an extension of the copyright page.

The African Poetry Book Series has been made
possible through the generosity of philanthropists
Laura and Robert F. X. Sillerman, whose
contributions have facilitated the establishment
and operation of the African Poetry Book Fund.

Library of Congress Cataloging-in-Publication Data
Names: Oriogun, Romeo, author.
Title: Sacrament of bodies / Romeo Oriogun.
Other titles: African poetry book series.
Description: Lincoln: University of Nebraska Press,
2020. | Series: African poetry book series | Poems. |
ISBN 9781496219640 (paperback: alk. paper)
ISBN 9781496220967 (epub)
ISBN 9781496220974 (mobi)
ISBN 9781496220981 (pdf)
Subjects: LCGFT: Poetry.
Classification: LCC PR9387.9.O747 S23 2020 |
DDC 821.92—dc23
LC record available at https://lccn.loc.gov/2019039054

Set in Garamond Premier by Laura Ebbeka.

For Dorcas Osadiaye, Lucy Omokha, and Yvonne Vera and to Kwame,

Chris, Matthew, and Bernardine for all the work and blessings.

In the one place everyone looks like me—
has my name—i am the most foreign.

—KAZIM ALI

CONTENTS

SACRAMENT OF BODIES

Before Your Mama Knew Us as Light

She took us to the house filled with letters facing east.
At first, we learned from the muezzin's call
the secret of sounds,
how it bends men into obedience.
I thought this is it, the way to stay alive
is to be silent,
is to imprison joy inside our bones,
a ritual born out of a ritual
meant to change the day into night.
You sat at the edge of the earth
to know if I meant deny the flesh.
We are dead in every world except this one wrapped
in blue. The man in a white gown washed the Arabic letters
for salvation into a bucket,
instructed us to wash ourselves clean of desire
and learn between words the gate through which God
took a bone and built a woman's body.
Before we learned to fight, we learned how to survive.
I watched you eat the sky, made it a miracle
that won't touch a woman's body,
maybe this is the way to rob God
or a means of walking back into your eyes
to be saved from what threatened to convert us into stones.
I watched you pass through my ribs,
a man nesting in the blood of another man,
this is wisdom made out of teeth
and bones and prayers drowning in water.
When we came out to say our final prayer,

the man took us into his arms,
passed our names through prayer beads to harden us
into men empty of the hunger to love in our language.
When he was done, I softened my name in milk
and prayed under the door.
May I find love in whatever body that gives me home. Amen.

The Ritual of Giving a Body Its Name

Who are we to give hunger a name?
The dog with hind leg raised to celebrate its victory
over the night calls to the wild,
the fearless, the ones not afraid
to be filled with lust or something
more than what the body hungers for.

But images in a broken mirror can be deceptive.

Take the fur covering a scar for example–
we know a trapped dog can chew its leg till it's free.
Say this is freedom, the price paid in perfect jars
filled with blood & bones.

Who are we to give what is heavier than blood a name?

We raised the mirror to our faces and begged it to show us magic,
to show us how to give our pagan desire a name
and it showed us the room with clothes scattered on the couch,
the semen-stained briefs, half-eaten granola bars,
spilled bottle of wine, red lake, red blood, skin,
the body begging to be touched gently
with a rod covered with blooming flowers,
to be opened into what is dried by desire
and it said, eat & be whole.

Cathedral of a Broken Body

In a room full of burning candles
I saw the man staring at me
and knew desire would drown
everyone standing between us
until we are the only two people alive.
After the music was over, after the girls
in the brothel went into their rooms,
I followed him home,
don't get me wrong, I didn't love him.
I wanted to know how a man begs for sex
till his thirst mirrors mine.
I sat on his chair and watched him,
his semen-stained sheet a map of lonely nights.
I want you; I don't know what we are doing here,
he kept saying.
High on marijuana, I didn't see the gun,
I didn't see his hand moving toward me.
All I knew was him calling my name
as if his desire was an ugly beast,
as if my face was the enemy.
I was afraid. The room became smaller,
his green army uniform was hanging
from a nail on the wall
as I went down on him.
He collapsed into my hands,
a baby seeing light for the first time
and all I did was caress his hair, closed my eyes
and swallowed his semen.

Departure

I do know about the hate that sinks a name
and turns water into homes drowning boys,
I cannot speak because my mouth is a grave.
Every day men hurting bodies filled with love
are praised as heroes,
are hailed as saviors opening bodies
into fields eaten by locusts.

I was born to be darkness hiding under a cave,
I know the weight of exile in a body.

The maestro said all art is full of departure.
I was born to hold a boy on a bus station,
shake him loose, a house leaking memories
and tell him go, run, live
until we meet again.

Tired of running, of drinking whiskey
in the afternoon to forget
the darkness you pushed me into.
I open my body into pain and bring out your words
faggot, sin, bones waiting for the tongue of fire.
I let them slice me, burn me.
I was born into a war. My God's duty is to hide
the honey dripping from my mouth.
I write the names of lovers leaving for Libya.
I let it grow on their tongues so they won't forget
how they lived in the dark before finding Agadez,
pathway, a road across the sea.

I worship the day because it survived the night.
I'm in a bus station
saying bye to boys searching for cities
where they can hold hands and walk on beaches.
I know what it means to live here,
with words invented for hate, with wounds asked to be silent.
And when they leave, I want to whisper into ears
filled with the fear of dying in the Sahara
do not forget I still live here.

Kumbaya

I cannot make this up.
Sunlight sneaks behind dark curtains

& you sit up, say the light is here again.

The streets hum with voices,
vehicles run into the rising sun,
my neighbor presses her ear against the wall
to hear the voice of heaven
falling from a mouth made beautiful by sin.
I want to find home in the rooms of your veins,
allow you to carry me as you flee into the day,

as you look back to stop your shadow from holding my hands.

In your room, your father smashes our bones against the wall,

our blood mingles, sings kumbaya as it streaks into the rug.

Tell me this is not love,
tell me this is not how couples run into sunsets.

Tell me this is not the universe saying love is eternal
to two bodies traveling through the sea as salt.

Your father digs me out of your stomach.

He says, no son of mine is going to be a faggot.

I allow light to preserve me, I allow it to slash me into songs
traveling through the forest softly as dew.

Here's my body, take it.

Here's my song searching for space within your lips,

open, sing it.

When they came for me with knives and sticks,

I became songs falling through rain.

Do not be afraid, I will always be here.
Just step into the wet sky,
open your mouth, sing,

sing, baby.

Saddest Night Alive

It always starts with your silence, with you running away,
even though you are here. The music is still playing
and all I want to do is dance, just to dance, baby,
but you are really not here. The sea is always hungry
and everyone is watching how you will feed it.
We are in a movie, we are acting
but you keep saying this is not right.
I want to know who made this desire so wrong.
The director is screaming, his veins are bulging,
I'm shouting leave him alone; they were the words I shouted
when they lynched you in my dreams.
My buttons undone and waiting for your fingers.
The leaves are falling,
It's the season for wearing new skin
and pretending you don't know this desire,
for pretending you didn't like the boy who rode across your mouth
last night and I understand you are afraid
because your friend's father gave him up to the police
on his birthday, and I know it's a shitty way to celebrate a new year
but I do not want to beg for your hands,
I do not want to steal into your dreams.
The DJ is playing another song,
bodies are moving like fireflies dancing by the riverside.
You are leaving. In my hand is a glass of gin and tonic.
I'm learning how to live with this fear of not finding love
in this city, how to watch my waves run back into the sea
like a dog cursed with the luck of finding dead lovers.
The director is shouting but you are already gone

and I'm leaving, drunk and in tears.
The music is still playing, still calling our hearts like clouds
waiting for the miracle of wings.
They will write this as the saddest night alive
but it won't mean a thing to us, we've been hurting
before the earth put to birth.

Elegy for a Burnt Friend

Because the night is silent,
the trees will search for a voice,
the wind will fill a body with sorrowful songs.
Forgive me, I drank old wine
as a mob marked your body.
There is nowhere to say enough,
nowhere to breathe in the open sea
without salt stinging your throat;
nowhere to wash our body in water and become free.
There was mockery on the spot
where your hand touched the blood on your shirt.
The voice said, you are fallen ashes, a mirror
of something unnatural, the dark side of God.
This was the point my mouth should have poured water
over your burning skin.
Forgive me, there was a pipe lying so close to another man;
there was a fire burning nearby and I ran into a dark street,
where I called your name in silence and said live,
knowing people like us will always be hunted.
I remember the night you licked the salt
in my palm and said do not be afraid to live in your skin.
Maybe you knew, you knew one day your scream
will stretch my throat and my silence will break
out of a darkness hard as a wall.

Coming Out

The woman on the bar stool knows your body
is a journey into songs,
the door into a moth flirting with fire,
which means there's a pretty boy
living under your skin.
I do not wish to come to you
but I can't help it,
you look drunk like a man
seeking a way out of himself
or a way into the beginning of his voice.
The city knows how to kill a man like you
and on the face of some men
I can see you burning.
Tonight, you take your first step into music,
saying your body knows how to beat a path
through hell and back,
saying angels do not die in song
you are daring like a throat accepting the fire of tequila.
Across from you in a dark booth, I want to scream
silently. *Do not dance,*
do not give in to the wild beat flowing through your heart.
But you are dancing like a boy drowning inside
his blood and all my body
can do is pray your soul into a bird's wings
and hope the wind calls you home.
Do you know the first thing about fire?
Have you seen a mouth calling God
only to find a body rising in smoke?

The city does not want
to hear your song flowing through a bird,
they don't want you dancing in the light.
Come into the dark before a man
greets your body with violence.
Come into the dark, let me sing
the night through your body
like a man learning how to worship God
in a strange land.

How to Survive the Fire

The first rule of survival is to run,
I tell you this so you understand how memories
are floods drowning a lonely man,
how the sight of a man burning
in a park stays with you;
his voice becoming yours at night.
There's no boy hiding in my throat.
I tell you the truth, my mouth is clean
but on my tongue are cities
where boys are beaten to death.
Say Lagos, say Onitsha, say Lafia,
say cities where the only freedom
for a man who loves another man is to leave.
I tell you this so you understand my silence,
understand why I crawled into my voice,
I do not want to die.
There is nowhere safe in this city of mine
and songs of freedom are just what they are.
You have to see nails drawing blood
from a swollen head
before you understand why God turned
his face from Christ and whispered, Run.

At Udi

We sat in our room
and watched *Paris Is Burning.*
A man hid himself between two cites,
gave up home, gave up the grace of a surname
to become himself.

We watched two men break it down
on the dance floor.
O the beauty, the sparkle,
the hands twisting through the air like music
rising from a piano.
A man said, *beauty, beauty, body, body.*

Under the light, I looked at my lover,
we were legendary. His hair was cut
into the latest fad, his shirt was vintage.
Lord, is beauty the only way
through which we can protest?
I'm tired of staying alive as a mannequin,
I want to be ugly
and still be heard.

My lover moved closer to the television,
he raised his hands to the ceiling
and said, *darling, I'm Labeija.*
I'm going to be a big fish
at the Lagos Fashion Week.

I kept quiet and watched him strut.
A bird flew away
from the balcony.
I walked up to him
and said, *the category is freedom, babe,*
freedom, not boredom, not beauty.

Denial

In the dark, my lover with a halo
offered his skin to me and said eat.
At night everything becomes a dream;
becomes real; becomes a dish.
The skin of a lover is a fish baked with olives,
in my mouth he multiplies.
When I was little my playmates
washed their fears into my soul and giggled.
There was no shame lying under my shirt
as I carried their stories into the eye of the sun.
Lover, I know tomorrow you will hide from me
as I walk across your shadow.
Do not try to explain, I dreamt there's always a beach
waiting for the souls of slain lovers.
It is a fact that we are born free
before tasting the fall of man.
When the sun is high there are a thousand men waiting
to mock my loneliness with pictures of death.
Tell me, what passes your lips as a mob
lynches my body into.
I want to remember you
as I fall out of your mouth
but my song reminds me of how you betrayed me
thrice in a room filled with angry men.
There's a part of me willing to forgive
but unlike Christ I can't find my voice.

The Guilt of Exile

In Café Pamplona, I sat down
to write
about my first pride march.

I can't recall the music
I danced to but my shirt still smelled
of the girl who hugged me
and said, *I'm a Christian, I'm sorry,*
forgive me.

On the train home,
I broke down in tears
as a friend commented on my picture,
your freedom is the hope I seek.
I do not know if I still have permission
to speak of the fear.
There was a cup of coffee on my table,
a couple shouted, *Happy Pride!*
Every night I reach for home
and fail. What is freedom
if a million people
still walk with the fear of being seen?

To the Man Who Mocked My Scared Body

Mala, we drowned in the morning
because they set our hair on fire.
Our tongues were heavy,
they laughed and watched us carry home
with our lovers on our shoulders while running into water.
Because I own no land that does not own me,
at night I'm not loyal to a city where a man bleeds.
I can ask why God's hands are full of dead boys
and walk out of a river.
In my sleep I'm always talking.
On the anniversary of our death
I let seven doves out of a cage,
we named them home and none returned.
I am always crying by the sink,
I don't know if it's my body mourning.
Can't you see the birds are burning
and there's no one to gather their bones?
O lost souls! O winds! Sing these bodies back to life.
Can't you see my hands blackened by burnt feathers?
Do not ask questions you already know the answers to.
I am hunted and not an animal running into hands created
by God or into a father with a knife hidden under his shirt.

Boy

He was born black and gay.
He was born in a house of light and flowers.
He thought freedom was a house painted
blue where a man played a guitar
until nightfall.
He held this hope as words in a prayer
until his mother walked from the old town
with her pastor's gospel of hell
filled with gay men.
He knew the price for walking away from home.
Only I knew his fears as he waited for his mother
to come home with the girl who she said held his cure.
Only I knew he cried as he couldn't touch the girl,
both of them naked in bed while his mother
stood by the door praying for him to be saved.
Only I knew the silence in their eyes,
creatures hungry for what their hands cannot provide.
Both of them grateful that I walked in,
grateful that I begged his mother to let him be.
You can never force home into a body already home.
His mother begged us into a ritual of silence
as the girl took a taxi home.

Pink Club

In the club at Garki, we dance in silence
because we are illegal, because the man
who tastes of gin also tastes of fear,
because the club is hidden in the eye of the night,
in a place where man dancing into another man
is a beautiful song humming deep within my veins,
I want to know heaven in the mouth of a boy
and we are crying because we are free,
because there's no sin inside dance,
because your father's voice is a far country
where sadness resides, call it home,
call it a place where boys who taste of flowers
are stolen at night.
You know sanctuary is where you run
into anyone that calls you home.
The drag queen dancing close to you
tastes of whiskey, you want to lie inside her,
close your eyes and walk away into her voice,
you want to fill your bones with wine
till a boy swims into your hands.
The bar sings of freedom, we keep wrecking it
because for once you are a butterfly
fluttering on the tongue of a boy
who called you beautiful.
I'm lying on a sofa because I'm dreaming
of cities filled with freedom,
because I'm free to drink pink gin from a pink bar.
Abuja sleeps because I'm free to raise

a city where boys who love other boys
are free to hold hands on the street.
You are laughing because this is strange,
because the first time you heard about this club
you thought about the boy who met love on Facebook,
who walked through his fear to meet a lynching
in a dark street, who couldn't report to the police
because a gay man is a fire waiting to happen.
Neon lights run along our limbs as we lose ourselves to dance,
the day is on my tongue, I'm tipsy,
all I want to do is sit before the sun
and drink rainwater on the skin of the boy
who called my mouth a city of refuge.

Before You Leave

Tell me about the dream where God stole you from your bed,
about the boy who wrote *faggot* under your name,
about your mama writing dead on your favorite picture,
about your street rising up in a wave to pound you into dust.

Tell me about the fear you hide under your oversized T-shirt.
You do not talk even when we sit in darkness
on the pier and watch as fishermen pull out grief
in the bodies of fishes. Under moonlight your skin
cracks into the finest black and I want to tell you
how sadness makes us lost and visible.

You remain silent even when comets
drop into water
and I know you are thinking
about being outed on Twitter,
about your house
buzzing with the word *forbidden*,
about the holy water waiting to chase
out the spirits singing under your skin.
You want to drink out of my happiness
and I'm happy to share but there's
this fear I hide in music,
when the radio plays a song filled with darkness
I want to lie in its mouth and get lost.

The tide is going out,
your head on my shoulder.
I know you must leave
because home has become a place
that eats the bones of young boys.

The Birthday

Memorize the shape of his face,
memorize the way his tongue
hangs out of his mouth.
Beat it into a sermon about death,
watch as he grows into an elegy hiding behind light.

There's a debate going on in my country:
Is fourteen years behind bars okay for a gay man
or should death be a better option?

There's no room to escape this hammer.
I know how it feels, how the world is a rope waiting
to hang you;
how every night you beg what roars inside you to be still.
I still want to believe that there's goodness left in this city
but they woke me up
and broke me and passed the law
that made me a criminal in my mother's home.

I could leave and no one will call my name at night,
in my hour of pain no one listens.

I've asked the sky to provide mist to protect
my first lover,
the one who still walks in shadows.

Tonight, a story is building,
do not expect a happy ending,

a boy is preparing a rope,
his body is purging a desire out of his blood,
his hands are holding the rope,
his mind is trying to forget
the moment a boy showed him
the meaning of bliss.
I've seen people die this way,
I've seen another type of mob
living in the head of a man
taught to hate what he yearns for.
I've seen how the city mocks everyone
that speaks a strange language.

On a tree there's a rope swinging
and a man is rising into the face
of God as what is rejected by a city.

I was born on a day like this.

A Viral Picture

I first saw the picture
on my friend's phone.
What escaped my throat was a sigh
and then silence.

There was a necklace made out of snails
on their necks,
the mob was swelling around them.
The short man in torn shorts
and swollen eyes was looking to the left,
his right hand was held by his lover.
I do not know their names,
but I know this is how we are still alive,
even with the scars and curses and fear,
we are still holding to each other,
we are still calling our names
and saying, we belong to this land.

My friend said, *let's pray for their souls to be saved.*
Lord, if my desire will stop me from coming into you,
I want to die in my truth.

There was almost a thousand people looking at this picture,
memorizing their faces, looking into their eyes,
asking, what is this desire?
Saying, they will never get a job in this city.

I kept looking into their faces,
into their swollen eyes.

Their bruises are all of us,
we are paying for our freedom
by walking naked,
by these men crying in a crowded street.

I am happy they are alive.
I am saying, we were broken,
our blood was spilled on sand,
still we rejoice that we are alive.

One day when we will come into the morning
and claim our land,
we will say, this is where we died, this is where we bled,
this is where we were homeless.
We have paid with everything we owned to be alive,
we will say, this is our city, this is our home.

Satan Be Gone

After Asa

The room smelled of sex, marijuana,
and cough syrup.
The soft voice of Asa
filled my ears.

He said, *blue birds are the children of the sea.*
I smiled, my foot tapping
to the rhythm of Asa's lyrics.

He whispered into my ear *Satan be gone.*
as he tried to find a way into my skin.
I tried to tell him I'm the beauty
of roads and rivers,
I tried to tell him I'm the feather of a bird
leading a man to drown under the sea.
His first bite was a man
learning the secret of soft words,
his second bite was a trip wire
in the breast of a man
learning how sex is a room
full of drugs where a man meets his fear.

He said, *Satan be gone,*
as he folded his tongue into my mouth,
as his fist found the softest part
between my ribs,
as I became the angel Jacob fought with
as he tried to find home between two names.

He said, *Satan be gone*,
as he cried in my mouth,
as he understood the beauty of the night,
as his fingers carved a memorial on my skin,
as my body became a womb
filled with blood and light
and a man finds the beginning of a journey
is also a door to fire.

He said, *Satan be gone*,
as his fist hit me again and again
before his body crawled into a wounded animal
at sleep,
as I staggered into water
and prayed that water and tears
would wash the blood flowing down my mouth.

What We Do Not Want

after Jennifer Perrine

We do not want the hate, no ghost boys wandering about cities that should be home, no sticks calling the name of love, no mother giving up on boys so soft the earth knows them as breath, no breaking of effeminate boys into houses filled with the pain of being strong, no song calling on the sky for fire, no fire speaking the language of burning skin, no empty rooms in the stomach of boys filled with love

&

we do not want you turning your back as queer boys are filled with straws, as they are made dry, as they are prepared to be sacrificed to a God whose body is filled with smoke, as they know fire as a ritual of death, as they know love as what leads to burnt bones, as they run into the dark to survive, as they navigate between shadows to know love, as they become used to their fingers searching for honey in a house without light, as they yearn for love, as they wander deep into questions that leave the body sore

&

we do not want the tears, no mother dragging us to church, no altar filled with the smell of burning incense, no prophet clad in a white gown, no Bible raised high like a sword, no whip coming down hard on bare backs, no boy holding his lover's name in a song of pain, no words of deliverance hanging over beautiful heads, no mother fighting back tears, no boy bathing with water filled with prayers and leaves, no boy walking back home with shame, no boy washing his tongue to be safe, no boy burning his skin to know the taste of death

&

we do not want pity, no eyes boring holes in our bodies, no eyes raising us into museum pieces, no boy mocking our bodies, no police officer arresting boys for love, no one asking how a kiss feels like, no one hitting batons on soft joints, no one giving us freedom because of bribes, no one opening our bodies into memories of storms, no one driving us out of our bones, no one scaring us with fourteen years in jail, no fear, nothing.

The Lost Chapter of the Bible Written after God Stopped Receiving the Smoke of Burnt Flesh

I.

I was asleep when the world was created. Every flower boy was called petal, our limbs were dance. Beauty lived in houses where we slept in peace and anointed our tongues with molasses. The earth was new, everyone was a lover, our nakedness was not seen. Tell me, what else does a body that will be endangered need?

2.

Every war starts with an invasion; it started like something unreal, a stone thrown through windows, two men beaten and made to walk through the village naked. We watched as a God was brought from a ship, we watched him become bigger, we watched him stop the dances, everyone became silent, his ritual was praise, we watched our tongues learn foreign words to please a God we couldn't hold. We watched and accepted ourselves as sin, we forgot our limbs and we became silent.

3.

The man in cassock was a fire. Hell is a body. We knew words could eat a body quicker than fire, we saw sons offered up as miracles to be hanged, to be lynched. Praise to our fathers for their silence. Praise to our fathers for giving us this gift of knowing the smell of hunters. Give them the gift of knowing the fear of a son leaving. Give them a lineage of boys hungry for a love that's as old as man. Amen.

4.

Before we forgot the gospel of love, they made our thumbs know the coldness of rosary beads as we walked away from ourselves. It is written that every thirst cannot be buried. How long did we stay confused, did we look at our bodies and call it darkness? How long did we shrink into a love that's not fully ours? Did we swallow our moans and became dead beings? Didn't they know that the body can't live in hiding forever? How long did they think we would keep licking our sweat to kill the wet dreams living in our nights?

5.

And the vision came to Femi under the orange tree, at a place where the hunger was greater than the fear and he turned to his people and said "a boy shall see another boy and he shall call the boy good, for his body was created to be love and he shall walk into this body and realize that this language was already his and the shame shall fall way away because love is love and he shall bring him to his father's house and they shall be one."

6.

And the vision traveled to every petal and we remembered and we woke up and became the world and the world became God and God became love and we poured colors into the air and created the rainbow, so they won't forget this history written in our tears.

Elegua

For the bird I set free to live

I bury the hunger to call a boy lover
and watch him grow into a bird
flying from death.

I let him go
and send a prayer after him
as I wash my pain in a sea full of memories.

I walk with a body afraid of light

in a nightclub where the DJ is God
creating worlds with sound
I retire into silence and allow the world to pass over me.

Afraid of someone asking for a cigarette
and finding a fabulous body dancing to Jimi Hendrix's song,
I drown glasses of rum and hide between neon lights.

Elegua, guide my coming out,
give me the power of walking between shadows and light.
Yemoja, send waves to wash away the blood waiting in dark corners.
every time I look up to the stage,
I feel someone raising a gun,
I must keep walking in the dark.

The Queer Boy Remembers Colonization

Sitting on the edge of a water reservoir
in southern Nigeria is as close as I can get to God.
The boys, lean like angels on their first day at work,
master the art of climbing.
Here, we know no one will defy gravity.
Here, we know the preacher gave us heaven
to forget the sadness of earth,
to forget our shoulders bearing the weight
of a man in a bowler hat.
We watch the city spread before us: Brown roofs with a history of British soldiers,
with a history of blood, with a history of a song birthing in the belly of women
as a monarch is sent on exile by men with common names like John,
James, men with names not filled with the myth of creation.
Who sends a God out of his kingdom
without knowing the weight of sorrow hidden in every mother at night?
Here, we can't escape every pain that comes with our lineage.
Here, the statues remind us of a long trek we can't run away from.
We see the priests coming out of water,
the baptism that led to a man taking up a name
that will never resemble him.
Death is only the body fulfilling its duty,
not a gateway to a promise made by a man
filled with the Holy Spirit.
Before night covers us, Bello begins the song
that comes from the bond of a mother to every child in this city.
We are not free, we know every flower
blooming here is an attempt to hide burnt homes.
We who are exiles in our homes,

who know the exit to every city,
who know every child born with the thirst
for a face like his must go into the forest
to begin a new city.
We who must join every song because music
carries home within its hands,
will join him. When we are done,
when the night becomes a blanket that doesn't hide our faces,
we will climb down and pray to survive this night
before they return with bayonets
to write a play where they will wear the faces
of white men and we will become gods,
sent to die in cities whose languages
won't hold the waters of our births.

Sacrament of Bodies

—After Chris Abani

It is true, the couch can't hold a boy ready to be split into love,
when we watch the rerun of movies
isn't it to tell our bodies that our desire won't kill us?
The light flickers, the hero is at the brink of death.
Take this piece of flesh, my finger in your mouth is a homily.
Remember the poor are those whose nights are filled with dreams of sailing.
Give to those who asked to be filled with light. Amen.
What do we know truly about darkness?
Resurrection is us walking into another room,
call it survival. Amen.
Every mass begins with surrender.
The flesh is holy like sex. Amen.
The tongue gives. The tongue receives.
Amen. Drink every river that knows our thirst.
Some Obelisks were erected to remember every savior
that walked through a city just like I walked through you.
Repeat the words. Bathrooms are sacred places
to know the inside of a lover.
Give the body what it deserves.
This is what it means to know God,
even if every God demands our death.
Moaning is knowing how a grave feels when it can't sing.
Amen. Rinse out every mouth that touched your lips,
for I am jealous. When I come, my vengeance
wrecks a body. Amen.
Keep my name in your mouth
for it is the doorway.

Watch as I fold the desire into a bed under the moon.
Every miracle is only a man
saying I will watch another moon show us
that the night is never truly dark.
For this is the way to finding the light.

I Do Not Want My Body to Fly

The sound of water running downhill is a lover in tears;
I do not understand the sin of leaving
but survival is a name I know intimately,

my head has turned away from your eyes
searching for me behind sunglasses.

Here you are, cupped palms creating a lake for my parched lips.
I wanted to be the hero in my story, so I held all the endings.
It is a selfish thing to behold God in your body

and call his name only in the dark, only when the door is shut behind you.
That's what I've done with your love.
Do you still see me as clouds, as water so pure
angels' wings were dipped in it before they could sing hosanna?

I told you I'm scared of burning,
I do not know enough to see the moment a man gives up on life.

I told you I'm scared of burning
because a burning man is so bright
it brings envy into the eyes of God.

Remember the first time we met in the town of red earth,
I watched you wear your sweatshirt, all I wanted to do was watch you
    forever
like God waking up every morning to watch the sunrise
because we are all guilty of vanity, because some skies are magic.
I told you about the man who walked on water.

I am sorry, that was not the story, here's the truth:
On the day he found water, he found my body.
I was full of grief; I was searching for my mother
in the painting on the wall.

The door was shut; he searched me for a window.
Okay, I promised to tell the truth.

He pushed me toward the wall;
his hand placed the sky without the sun under my skin.
He laughed when I ran away.
Do you know the room where thunder sleeps?

Last night after you left, I dreamt my blood was a dirty river.
You didn't want to drink it. The truth is you called me a pool cursed to suffer
and that's how I understood love, a kind of punishment.

What do you say to a body always flying?
Do not cry, home will never be enough for me.

The truth is always a house with many windows; I wanted you to hold my wings,
pluck out every fear and leave me whole because I do not want my body to fly
from your eyes, I want the risk of burning; I want to know you before dawn.

Here you are, walking away again; I am sorry we speak different languages.
I am going to watch you leave
and walk in your footsteps; this is also love,
the need to touch memories
and see in my tears a lover walking home.

My Body Is No Miracle

Before I discovered home I sat on a beach to hear the water
in me speak to the water going back into places I've never been to.

I want to tell you about my voice dissolving in water,
getting lost because I hid it from my father
who pretended to be asleep when I called the boy who spoke Portuguese on the phone.

And nothing gets better, not the boys setting fire to your doll's hair,
not your mother asking where you learnt that language from,
where you got the magic to make boys drop like dead leaves behind you.

You do know some songs play forever, do not forget
the boy who you thought understood will say at night,
I don't want you touching me, no funny business here.
And you will grow smaller, dirtier, you will stay awake
because you don't want your body moving on his own.
The morning won't bring smiles, your father's phone call
will be a bullet, the exact size that shatters bones.

There is no place where you will be accepted,
even God has moved out of you
and it is all right because you will search for cast-offs
like you, souls filled with love in dark places,

souls who knew how home is also war.
You will raise a house together from darkness,
from love, from all the words that have thrown
you into the cold and there will be no gospel there,

just the boy who begged God to take away this thirst,
the boy whose mother burnt his five fingers,
the boy who couldn't believe light
is somewhere you lie down and sleep without
searching for blows, the boy who knew nothing but darkness.
You will sing these beautiful bodies to sleep.

I do not know when I became saved,
when my body knew life exists without tiptoeing
around my father's house, praying he doesn't hear our giggles,
praying my love won't wake the anger resting in his fist.
I do not know when I started saying things I felt like saying,
there was no miracle to my salvation, just a boy walking on a lonely road,
walking into other boys who knew salvation lies in raising a home in the wild.

My Tinder Date Speaks of Fruits

I have never been afraid to place a bowl of fruits on the tongue of a river.

If this is how a son pleases a mother,
then call me good,
call me the light that refuses the allure of the night.

My Goddess is what inhabits the bottom of the sea,
say this is a better way to hide.

The girl behind the wheels laughed when she spoke of queer boys,
she said, *Haiti knows how to kill boys that are too soft,*
she said, *on D Street in Boston, Fruits walk with swinging buttocks,*
all they want is a man for the night,
she asked, *why are you not laughing?*

The boy at the back began a story with the broken bones of queer boys.
He said, *at Atlanta we beat up some fruits the night we had some rum at the club,*
we fucked them up, we say be gay but don't slice through the day to show us.
I opened a hole in his back to bring out my mouth.

I'm Bisexual and Black.
I was born between two cities in a river without language.

When my aunt speaks to me on the phone,
her voice sounds like a translation.
I am without proverbs to be Yoruba.
I am without cowries to be Benin.
What hides me is what pushes me away.

I envy everything with a home.
Do you know the best death is by a door?
At least what doesn't call you son will bury you.

What I am is an empty body,
a song without a sound,
I own no place to call love.

In church the pastor said, *heaven is home for whomever throws the first stone,*
meaning God sanctioned the cutlass to know the thirst of blood,
meaning every son disowned for what shouts under his skin is without God.

In everywhere I'm called sin, I seek to be free.

Before Brookline she dropped me by the road side,
gave me the finger, and drove away.
I turned to the wind,
to what is without form
and this too is how the earth becomes home
for a body creating a room from every rejected breath.

A Reversed Epithalamium or
What Didn't See the Light

We had planned for a quiet wedding,
somewhere in the forest,
beneath the tree where my mother was buried
because what didn't die happy must be offered libations.
One time we were in bed, a bottle of rum
on the bedside table, two half-empty glasses beside it,
our naked bodies a mass of happiness
and she turned to ask, "Isn't this body glorious enough to stop you
from longing after a boy?"
I looked at her, two eyes, two lamps carved out of the dark
and I wanted the darkness also.
I couldn't explain to her why a boy's mouth
just like hers can be a fisherman paddling my boat to shore.
It is over now. Her, tired of holding her skin
against every boy my shadow touches.
I, tired of holding my body in the light,
begging to be seen.
Yesterday I visited my mother's grave,
the tree has been cut down
and I saw a doe staring at me from afar.
In my room, a tuxedo sits in the closet like a man
staring at an empty street from a window.

Heaven Is a Back Alley without God

Where we hide to count the stars.
Sometimes a Pastor walks through the wooden houses
at night to find solace in a boy,
to cover a boy with his hands
before calling him sin on Sunday.
Sometimes a boy walks back home
to know where the fire is still burning,
to see the scars under a lamp,
to call a hand behind the whip father,
to spell his name on the wall with blood.
I've seen a man pouring drops of water
into the mouth of another man
to know God is never coming to save us,
but we make do with what we've been given, this slice
of earth, this room with rainwater finding holes in roofs,
this boy calling another boy the night, this darkness that hides us,
this desire to find a way home in the dark,
this gutter full of rats and sewage.
Hide the glitter on my skin, I say to the day
as I walk through the city's eye.
I know what the dying think, *what God is wide enough*
to fold my body close to his heart.
I know what the living think, *this hope*
stopping me from leaving is not a miracle.
I know what the man hitting the boy thinks,
who chose to be poor and queer?
At night I return home to this place that speaks my language,
a car stops to pick a boy by the junction, the man behind the wheel

might be a politician, might be one of the hands
that signed the law to call us evil.
What doesn't call us home during the day finds us at night.
Father, it hurts, the beauty of the knife,
the ways it finds a path through skin,
the stones raining down on us, our voices never calm enough
to call peace to a river. Here, heaven is not safe enough
to sing hallelujah, behind a house a boy carves his name
on a wall with unsteady hands to tell the world a body full of glory
is also full of fear.

Goodbye

For Jephthah

I have forgotten the feeling of pain leaving a body,
the way the hand waved goodbye as if walking
into what won't leave it whole.
Maybe that's why sad songs leave us empty,
maybe that's why I didn't complain after you poured tea
into my cup about its sweetness
because even when leaving, love is still sharp enough
to bleed a man to death.
I touched your hand, not knowing the gift I had touched,
I let it go, not knowing what it is
I had let go. I watched you smile,
not knowing what was dying.
The distance between us stretched to Minna.
I searched for you as the car stopped by the city wall,
the way a man searches for air and fails.
I searched for you in the language of blood and sand
this place was built upon.
Every lean man in a caftan walking toward me
felt like you but you were not there.
I know in every language there's a hole
that a word cannot fill. I've hid you there,
knowing the gift I had lost, knowing you are so fragile,
knowing a man must love a word
so much to give it a new name to fill the hole
on his tongue.

Exile

There's a gift I was given,
a horse with its broken legs.
Lord, I tend to this brief thing called life like a man
caring for a beast that eats what it loves.
I can't help this loneliness of people walking away from my eyes,
it is how a city knows its walls have fallen.
The plane breaks through the clouds & San Juan comes into view,
this city shall survive this water, I say.
Once I knew where my circle was in the world,
I could walk into forests with just a book & find my way
back to my mother's chest.
I should tell you, my mother's chest was a tree,
beside it a flower blossomed and was called grace.
I should tell you, I once saw the river drown a bone,
maybe this is death, maybe this is a mother welcoming a son.
The driver says welcome and I know he means stranger,
I know he means what drives you into the world.
I have come here to find what I'd lost but it will spit me out,
a seed floating on water, a boat, a life
without the luck of trees.
The city stretches into a fort, as if it is still ready for war,
as if a battleship sits eternally before her eyes.
I have known this fear, it is called reaching into the future for the cut,
meaning I still see the men who called me *homo*, meaning dirt,
meaning sin, meaning their hands shall divide my body into a barren field.
I once woke up to the beast in my chest cage,
I held it tenderly before severing its neck.

My therapist called it a sacrifice,
meaning I saw the blood even in the dark,
I smelled it and knew home drowned last night.
Father, here is what I was given, a goat, the beauty to walk back to the knife,
the man saying grace as if blood isn't pure enough
and this city. Here at night, I will walk into anything that calls me home,
it will hold me for a while. I've seen my mother's bed this way,
the burgundy color of the bedsheets, the walls with old photographs,
her skin. Here my mother is alive, she's my city
and I hold her close. Mother, stay with me for a while,
stay before the sea comes to wash us clean of our thirst.

Battle of the Rams

The field has ceased to be lush wonder, from the eyes of a bird I watched them go again and again, horns finding the softness behind fur. Here, what seek for death is been praised. Young boys jump into the air to know the weightlessness of joy. Every year they come here to know death, to know the last sound of a dying animal is a plea for the knife. I looked from above, sending back the spirit of dead animals into the bodies of little boys. We were never too young to know the tongues of kites are beginnings to rituals and when these boys begged to be set free from seeing a horn spill blood on grasses, what do they mean? We all must know death to know the sadness of a grave.

Again, another ram is led to the center, a whistle is heard, another ram is allowed to walk through. The sun kept shining, faithful witness to every war, to every broken horn, to every animal whispering for death. Another ram is fallen. Abdul turned to me, the knife in his hand ready to run through the ram's neck is an act of mercy.

This is the ritual of war I was given. In a train in Boston I tried to hide in a book while an old woman kept saying *I write for Africa*, as if Africa is a little bowl of water, as if our tongues are not divided by borders. She turned to me to say *you must know about conflict zones*. Even when invisible, I am asked about the origin of war. I opened my palm to spill a ram's blood on her seat. This is what I know, a ram will look death in the eye and run toward it just like a man walking into the night with the weight of a continent on his back.

Finding Home

Behind a broken-down car,
A boy hides.
I tell this story & believe hiding could save me
from the world, from my mother
who would say spell the words written on the cupboard,
each letter an attempt to distract me from the whip,
from her tears, from her hand that held love and pain in a fist,
from kisses she would plant on my cheek
after a fight filled with glasses of whiskey.
Here I am, a horse standing outside a shack, an animal racked with pain.
The smell hits me, all these years what was I running from?
A butterfly flutters close to a flower, a boy in a red shirt releases a pigeon
from a wooden cage, beauty exists in every gesture, in my mother's face
turning to catch the last light of the day,
in the scars along her belly, in the way her smiles
forgive me for leaving,
in the way a pigeon forgives the tree
by returning to perch on a limb.
Close to death some prisoners sing as if blood will heal every trauma
they are leaving behind, yet the price of sin does not make a body whole.
I say this and a man stands over me. What do you remember?
Everything a body should forget.

What the World Won't Show Us

to my mother without the baby

Of the many people singing tonight, you are the loneliest, although you buried a child and hid a pig's skin beside your bed, something to remind you of a baby's warmth. Behind the house a bird sings from a guava tree and here again is the language of grief, every song is a door calling us to the past and what gives when our voice can't hold a name? The gospel speaks of love as clay opening the eye of a blind man, but love is also you, rubbing clay on your skin to trap a name. Tonight, you bit into desire to hide your pain and called the process gifting a lover a body. Mother, what doesn't share of our grief is not of us. The horse hooves hitting the ground is a question to the past, a means of breaking the earth into a room to see the cup of pomade sitting on the chair, a hot comb passing through bristled hair. Even in this moment, holy is the son ready to hit the grave, holy are hands holding the satin gown, holy are the wings holding back the sun, holy is a brother holding another brother. Mother, what is the child's name? This I know is what you seek in every lover. In the dark, the night was once quiet, so was I, so was the child crying across the field.

On Forgetting

I walked and walked
and no one called my name.
I cannot remember the time
or the date they died.
I only have their graves
to remind me of their absence.
I only have the lullaby
to remind me that my father
once held my hand
and called me beautiful.
I walked toward Ikpoba Bridge,
there I asked the man drinking
beer by the riverside, *do you remember*
the man and woman who met here,
can you recall their faces?
What does it mean to forget love, to forget home?
A stray dog barked
before running into the bush,
what is lost always sees
what is running away.
I sat by the roadside and watched the cars
pass me by. Remembering is a pilgrimage.

Everything Must Die

After Natasha Tretheway

2003, I just knew that death had no voice
to reach back to us.
Moving houses and registering in an evening school
was a way of leaving what won't come with us.
I cried as the dusty roads stripped us
of every privilege we own,
the evenings were getting stretched into masses
filled with silence and there was no benediction
when I found it, the dog with a house of fleas in its fur,
the dog I named Benny and held close to me
as I picked every flea and left its fur
brown like a ripe field of corn.
The boys in the yard laughed at my softness
and threw stones at Benny,
they thought a dog with one eye was a wizard,
they laughed at his gait
until the night when he couldn't sleep,
when his voice was a lesson in lamentations.
The night knew what left and when we walked into the morning,
we saw him, Efe, one of us, child of the street,
his hand outstretched like a compass needle
pointing to the north as if he knew the way
before the bullet found him.
I had seen death once: my father slept on the couch
like a child walking back to life and forgot his way.
I had known silence, the way it follows us
when we are not looking

but the second death we know
is the death of our innocence,
and Benny died when they poisoned him.
I held him and cried for everything dead inside of me,
including a father whose smell I won't recognize.

On the 23rd Death Anniversary of My Father

My body reaches down into a bottle of gin
to make a world out of something close to death.
We were never meant to be alive,
to be 25 and a chandelier broken
into a million fragments of light.
Father allowed the bees to escape from the beehive.
Here's the sting, here's the sound of fear,
here's your father's face carved into the day
breaking the world across your back,
here's all his memories burning down your bones.
The wound hurts in its softest part.
During the war a father saved the severed head
of his daughter, he talked to it until a rotten
head talked back.
Here's your father's head in your bosom,
here's your mouth begging for love,
for his tongue to show you a way home.
Here's your father saying you can't teach
a dead man how to love.
All the rivers come into you,
which means water is never enough
to save a man falling from the sky.
I have learnt to love every broken thing
the way a man learns to live with a memory that doesn't die.
I have learnt to carry my father's body in my heart like a son
that inherits a knife cut without flinching.

Prelude to Freedom

At the hospital, the man on the chair
said, there's a child trapped in your past,
you have to let him go.
I am walking into my past,
the women by the river are weaving baskets,
a cousin is washing clothes on a brown stone.
Father, I am trying hard to be a man.
Your corpse is lying in the living room,
I didn't tell my siblings the drugs you took
was you saving us from seeing the illness eat you.
I, who have walked all my life with the illness
I inherited from you. I, who have blamed all your anger
on something else have come to know you
from the journals you left behind.
The doctor once asked if I blamed you
for the wars I carry within me
and I kept quiet because I wanted to say yes again
but I have read your words and knew I am walking
in your path, every day it hurts, every day the world
mocks me.
Father, I must write about my pain
and about yours, maybe, just maybe I am saving myself
from how the world trapped you
in a strength that stopped you
from seeking help.
Maybe I am crying to the world
to let me watch the sunrise with you
one more time without calling up
this history of finding salvation
in every destruction you left behind.

Sermon of Pain

At the grave, the dead sang hosanna.
Praise to the man, to the body found wanting.
Praise to strangers holding you.
Pain travels to return.
Praise to scrubbed hospitals,
to my mother's body perfectly opened like a fruit.
Praise to scalpels, to lines that divide a stomach,
to the dead baby, to the name I whispered,
to God, to seven decades of rosaries,
to empty pharmacies, to the doctor who blamed the Government,
to the Government who blamed the dollar,
to the dollar who blamed corruption.
Praise to poor bodies too heavy for airplanes,
praise to foreign hospitals,
praise to money, praise to exhaustion,
to dust to dust, to sand hitting dead breasts,
to silence, to calling a body, to grief.
Praise to knowing it is over,
praise to nakedness,
to pain, to my tears, to turning back on a body,
to calling it nothing, to know death, to call it mother,
to the waiting, to the sermon, to God has called his own,
to holy selfishness, to rob the poor,
to call pain holy, to be lost, to say amen,
to say fuck you, to break down, to know nothing
to walk under the rain, to call everywhere mother,
to know pain is a sound, to listen to silence,
to give it a name, to call it death, to call it nothing,
to call it mummy, to call it God.

Meeting My Mother through Death

Nineteen years after my father's death,
I will search for my mother's picture
in the portmanteau where he kept the memories
that must not see the light.
In the dark I will let my fingers
hold pieces of the dogoyaro tree
that stands over my buried placenta,
I will touch the rough surface
of the bong pipe he hid before dying
and see a man falling slowly into a grave.
I will pass the last blanket he had, the letters
my half-brother held tenderly before filling with postage stamps
I will pass the marriage certificates,
the cobwebs settling over the signatures
of my parents, the court papers that broke them apart,
then I will pull her picture out of the dark.

In her picture is a room. I will walk into it
and kneel beside a chair, as the photographer raises his head
over his Polaroid to nod to her,
as if a nod is the magic to trap a face in time.
I will watch the wind from the window lift her skirt
and see the storm underneath, the scars she hid
with prayers in the bathroom,
the blows, her face turning away as a hand becomes a fist,
the bus station, the goodbye that was not said,
and when the light blinds our eyes
I will call a name that was not given to me

and whisper, *Mother, I love a man the same way I've loved a girl.*
I am afraid I might see her flinch
and won't know if it's from the light
or from words that cut deeper
into every wound her body has ever known.

After a Blackout

The body coming into a morning
does not mean it is healed.
Remember the turning of the key,
how I saw light and thought this is the end
because like the dead I couldn't piece together time
and give it a meaning
but the girl with the tattoo on her right wrist,
who took me to a homeless shelter
just before a Chinese restaurant
said I danced as if I knew every song had a door,
said I called a flower the gateway and waited.
Perhaps the body before dying becomes a bee,
becomes what knows sweetness intimately.
I woke up in a chair,
not knowing how many lost bodies it has given home
but I was grateful to see the sunrise,
grateful to see Charles River flow by,
even if I know water says one thing,
the land says another
and those trapped between them
become a body filled with sand and water.
They called me drifter, after a wood,
after a man with a sign at Harvard Square that says *Help! I'm Alive.*
Those who still have a voice still have hope,
still know a place is home, still know the road is just a road.
The girl said her name is Haley, I didn't offer my name,
didn't know what body I woke up in
but I was grateful for the cigarette she offered,
grateful that we smoked in silence, the smoke finding the sky
like an offering of burnt doves for the gift of another day.

ACKNOWLEDGMENTS

Thank you to the following journals where some of the poems first appeared.

Agbowo: "What We Do Not Want"

Brittle Paper: "Departure," "Kumbaya," "Saddest Night Alive," "Satan Be Gone"

McNeese Review: "My Tinder Date Speaks of Fruits"

Prairie Schooner: "My Body Is No Miracle"

Praxis: "Boy"

Up the Staircase Quarterly: "What the World Won't Show Us"

Fuchsia
Mahtem Shiferraw

Your Body Is War
Mahtem Shiferraw

In a Language That You Know
Len Verwey

Logotherapy
Mukoma Wa Ngugi

When the Wanderers Come Home
Patricia Jabbeh Wesley

*Seven New Generation African
Poets: A Chapbook Box Set*
Edited by Kwame Dawes
and Chris Abani
(Slapering Hol)

*Eight New-Generation African
Poets: A Chapbook Box Set*
Edited by Kwame Dawes
and Chris Abani
(Akashic Books)

*New-Generation African Poets:
A Chapbook Box Set (Tatu)*
Edited by Kwame Dawes
and Chris Abani
(Akashic Books)

*New-Generation African Poets:
A Chapbook Box Set (Nne)*
Edited by Kwame Dawes
and Chris Abani
(Akashic Books)

*New-Generation African Poets:
A Chapbook Box Set (Tano)*
Edited by Kwame Dawes
and Chris Abani
(Akashic Books)

To order or obtain more information on these or other University of
Nebraska Press titles, visit nebraskapress.unl.edu. For more information
about the African Poetry Book Series, visit africanpoetrybf.unl.edu.